STARTING OUT

CREATIVE EDUCATION • CREATIVE PAPERBACKS

PUBLISHED BY CREATIVE EDUCATION AND CREATIVE PAPERBACKS

P.O. Box 227, Mankato, Minnesota 56002
Creative Education and Creative Paperbacks
are imprints of The Creative Company
www.thecreativecompany.us

LIBRARY OF CONGRESS CATALOGING-IN-PUBLICATION DATA

Names: Riggs, Kate, author.
Title: Baby penguins / Kate Riggs.
Series: Starting out.
Summary: A baby penguin narrates the story of its life, describing how physical features, diet, habitat, and familial relationships play a role in its growth and development.

Identifiers: ISBN 978-1-64026-078-8 (hardcover)
ISBN 978-1-62832-666-6 (pbk)
ISBN 978-1-64000-194-7 (eBook)
This title has been submitted for CIP processing under LCCN 2018939097.

CCSS: RI.K.1, 2, 3, 4, 5, 6, 7; RI.1.1, 2, 3, 4, 5, 6, 7; RF.K.1, 3; RF.1.1

DESIGN AND PRODUCTION

by Chelsey Luther and Joe Kahnke
Art direction by Rita Marshall
Printed in the United States of America

PHOTOGRAPHS by Alamy (Photononstop, Steve Bloom Images), Getty Images (Thomas Kokta/Photolibrary, Gerard Lacz/Visuals Unlimited, Inc., Michael S. Nolan/age fotostock), iStockphoto (AntAntarctic, KeithSzafranski), Minden Pictures (Stefan Christmann/BIA, Klein and Hubert), National Geographic Creative (IRA MEYER, Paul Nicklen, JOEL SARTORE/NATIONAL GEOGRAPHIC PHOTO ARK), Shutterstock (Potapov Alexander, Bohbeh, Eric Isselee, Schnapps2012, TravelMediaProductions)

FIRST EDITION HC 9 8 7 6 5 4 3 2 1
FIRST EDITION PBK 9 8 7 6 5 4 3 2 1

baby PENGUINS

KATE RIGGS

ENTS

I AM A CHICK.

I am a baby penguin.

eye

down feathers

I came out of an egg.
It took three days to
break my shell!

My **down** feathers are soft. But I will need different feathers before I can swim.

I am a different color from my parents.

They fish for food in the sea. We eat <u>krill</u>, squid, and fish.

tongue

My tongue has <u>spines</u>.

It helps me hold on to slippery fish!

All my down is gone. Now my feathers are waterproof.

I am a young penguin!

SPEAK AND LISTEN

SQU

SQAAAWK!

Can you speak like a baby penguin? Penguins call, sing, and squawk.

Listen to these sounds:

https://www.youtube.com
/watch?v=BVMzjiOUpZo

Now it is your turn!

CHICK WORDS

down: fluffy feathers that form the first covering of baby birds

krill: small shrimplike animals found in the oceans

spines: pointy parts that stick out

READING CORNER

Dinmont, Kerry. *It's a Penguin!* Minneapolis: Lerner, 2019.

Idzikowski, Lisa. *How Penguins Grow Up*. New York: Enslow, 2017.

Terp, Gail. *Penguins*. North Mankato, Minn.: Black Rabbit Books, 2017.

INDEX